Songbirds

# Sue Kangaroo

Story by Julia Donaldson
Pictures by Daniel Postgate
Series editor Clare Kirtley

OXFORD
UNIVERSITY PRESS

3

# Tips for reading Sue Kangaroo together

This book practises these letter patterns:

oo  ew  ue  o  (all pronounced *ue* as in *blue*)

Split vowels: a–e  i–e  o–e  u–e

Ask your child to point to these letter patterns and say the sounds (e.g. *oo* as in *kangaroo*). Look out for these letter patterns in the story.

Your child might find these words tricky:

can't  dinner  her  here  out  Mrs  says  some
teacher  the  there  tomorrow  what  your

These words are common, but your child may not have learned how to sound them out yet. Say the words for your child if they do not know them.

Before you begin, ask your child to read the title. Remind your child to read words they do not recognise by sounding out and blending. Look at the picture together. What do you think this story is about?

- Ask your child, *Did Sue like school? How do you know?* (Yes, because she says 'Hooray' when she finds out that there is school tomorrow too.)
- On pages 20 and 21 find some words which rhyme (*Sue, glue, too*). Point to the letter pattern that makes the long *ue* sound in the words (*ue, oo*). On page 22 find more words which contain a long *ue* sound (*school, rules, Drew* ). Point to the letter pattern that makes the long *ue* sound in each word (*oo, u–consonant–e, ew*).

4

This is school

and this is Sue

and this is
Mummy Kangaroo.

The teacher's name is Mrs Drew.

She says hello to Mum and Sue.

"This is Sue," says Mrs Drew.

"Do be kind to her. She's new."

"Time to paint," says Mrs Drew.

Sue says, "I like red and blue."

"Time to glue," says Mrs Drew.

"Sue can glue a kangaroo!"

"Dinner time," says Mrs Drew.

"This is yummy stew," says Sue.

"Music time," says Mrs Drew.

"I can play the spoons!" says Sue.

"Home time soon," says Mrs Drew.

"But what is in your pocket, Sue?"

Sue takes out a tube of glue.

She takes some spoons and
paint out too.

"The school has rules," says Mrs Drew.

"You can't take those things home with you."

Sue is sad. "Don't cry," says Prue.

"Play with them tomorrow, Sue."

"Is there school tomorrow too?"

"Is that true? Hooray!" says Sue.

Here is Mummy Kangaroo.
"Hi, Mum! School is cool!" says Sue.

Songbirds

# The Cinderella Play

Story by Julia Donaldson

Pictures by Ross Collins

Series editor Clare Kirtley

OXFORD

UNIVERSITY PRESS

# Tips for reading The Cinderella Play together

This book practises these letter patterns:

ee  y  e  (all pronounced *ee* as in *three*)

igh  ie  y  i-e  (all pronounced *ie* as in *tie*)

o-e  o  (all pronounced *oe* as in *toe*)

ay  a-e  a  (all pronounced *ai* as in *train*)

oo  ew  o  (all pronounced *ue* as in *blue*)

s  ss  se  ce  c  (all pronounced *s* as in *seen*)

er  (pronounced *er* as in *over*)

Ask your child to point to these letter patterns and say the sounds (e.g. *ay* as in *play*). Look out for these letter patterns in the story.

Your child might find these words tricky:

danced  door  dropped  have  her  liked  picked  said  some  the

they  was  were

These words are common, but your child may not have learned how to sound them out yet. Say the words for your child if they do not know them.

Before you begin, ask your child to read the title. Remind your child to read words they do not recognise by sounding out and blending. Look at the picture together. What do you think this story is about?

When you have finished reading the story, look through it again and:

- Ask your child, *Why did the ugly sisters try on a boot?* (Because Fred had lost the slipper.)

- Find and read some words on page 54 which begin with a *s* sound (*cinema*, *said*). Point to the letter pattern that makes the *s* sound (*c*, *s*).

30

The twins were in a play.

It was a play of Cinderella.

Mum and Dad came to see it. Gran came too.

Fred was the prince. He had to
sing a song.

Flick was a goose. She had to hiss at the ugly sisters.

The ugly sisters were bossy. They made Cinderella do the dusting.

Cinderella had an old dress and a duster.

But then she got a nice new dress.

She got some silver slippers too.

Cinderella went to the palace.

She danced with the prince.

But then she ran away. She dropped a silver slipper.

The prince picked it up.

Cinderella ran home. Her ugly sisters went home too.

Cinderella had her old dress on.

The prince had to knock on the door.

He had to try the slipper on Cinderella and her sisters.

But Fred had lost the slipper!
"Have my boot!" said Miss Hill.

The ugly sisters tried on the boot.

It was too loose. But they said, "It's too tight!"

Cinderella tried on the boot.
It was too loose. But she said, "It fits!"

Mum and Dad liked the play.

"It was better than the cinema!"
said Gran.

Songbirds

# Usman's Books

Story by Julia Donaldson

Pictures by Martin Chatterton

Series editor Clare Kirtley

OXFORD

UNIVERSITY PRESS

55

# Tips for reading Usman's Books together

This book practises these letter patterns that all make the same sound:

## oo   oul   u

Ask your child to point to these letter patterns and say the sound (e.g. *oo* as in *books*). Look out for these letter patterns in the story.

Your child might find these words tricky:

## ball   basket   football   her   some   the

These words are common, but your child may not have learned how to sound them out yet. Say the words for your child if they do not know them.

Before you begin, ask your child to read the title. Remind your child to read words they do not recognise by sounding out and blending. Look at the picture together. What do you think this story is about?

When you have finished reading the story, look through it again and:

- Ask your child, *What would Usman like to do? Why?* (Step into his books to meet the characters.)

- On pages 62 and 63 find some words which contain the vowel sound *oo* as in *book (could, put, would, cook, good, pudding)*. Point to the letter pattern that makes the vowel sound *oo* in these words *(oul, u, oo)*. Think of some other words which contain the vowel sound *oo* (e.g. *hook, push, full)*.

My name is Usman. This is
my bookshelf.

I like reading my books.

I wish I could step into a book!

# If I could step into this book...

I would meet a cook.

I could put a hat on too

and we would cook a good pudding.

# If I could step into this book...

I would meet Red Riding Hood.

I could help her carry her basket

and I could help the
woodcutter rescue her.

# If I could step into this book...

I would meet Puss in Boots.

I could pull on some boots too

and I would chase mice with him.

If I could fly into this book…

I would meet a spaceman.

I could put on a helmet too

and we would whoosh to the
moon in a rocket.

If I could run into this book...

I would meet a football team.

We would play football and I would
kick the ball into the goal.

And if *you* could step into
this book…

you would meet me!

Songbirds

# The Upside-down Browns

Story by Julia Donaldson

Pictures by Sam McCullen

Series editor Clare Kirtley

**OXFORD**
UNIVERSITY PRESS

# Tips for reading The Upside-down Browns together

This book practises these letter patterns that all make the same sound:

**ow   ou**

Ask your child to point to these letter patterns and say the sound (e.g. *ow* as in *Brown*). Look out for these letter patterns in the story.

Your child might find these words tricky:

**are   comes   have   her   Mr   Mrs
the   their   they   two**

These words are common, but your child may not have learned how to sound them out yet. Say the words for your child they do not know them.

Before you begin, ask your child to read the title. Remind your child to read words they do not recognise by sounding out and blending. Look at the picture together. What do you think this story is about?

When you have finished reading the story, look through it again and:

• Ask your child, *Why are Mr and Mrs Brown funny?* (They do strange things such as read the paper upside down and go to town in their dressing gowns.)

• Read pages 90 and 91. Find some words which contain a long *ow* sound (*cloudy, out*). Point to the letter pattern that makes the long *ow* sound in the words (*ou*). Think of some words which rhyme with *out* (e.g. *shout, spout, sprout*).

Mr and Mrs Brown read the paper upside down.

Mr and Mrs Brown have a teapot with two spouts

and coffee comes out of their taps.

Mr and Mrs Brown have a funny round house.

It spins round and round like
a roundabout.

Mr Brown puts on his trousers to have a shower.

He blows his nose on a towel.

He puts on his sun hat when it is cloudy.

He takes it off when the
sun comes out.

Mrs Brown is funny too.

She bounces around in a crown.

She puts flour on her nose

and she puts powder in the cakes.

Mr and Mrs Brown go to town in their dressing gowns.

They climb mountains in their slippers.

They grow flowers in their bed.

And they sleep outside in the
flower bed.

And when Mr and Mrs Brown
see a clown...

they frown!

But if you think Mr and Mrs Brown
are funny . . .

how about their pets?

# Songbirds

# Leroy

Story by Julia Donaldson
Pictures by Jess Mikhail
Series editor Clare Kirtley

OXFORD
UNIVERSITY PRESS

# Tips for reading Leroy together

This book practises these letter patterns:

**oi oy (all pronounced *oi* as in *coin*)**

**le (pronounced *le* as in *middle*)**

Ask your child to point to these letter patterns and say the sounds (e.g. *oy* as in *boy*). Look out for these letter patterns in the story.

Your child might find these words tricky:

**all brother her isn't one says sometimes the there what**

These words are common, but your child may not have learned how to sound them out yet. Say the words for your child if they do not know them.

Before you begin, ask your child to read the title. Remind your child to read words they do not recognise by sounding out and blending. Look at the picture together. What do you think this story is about?

When you have finished reading the story, look through it again and:

- Ask your child, *Why don't Granny and Grandpa think Leroy is annoying?* (Because they don't know what he is really like.)
- Find some words on pages 120 and 121 which contain a long *oi* sound (*Leroy, annoys, noisy*). Point to the letter pattern that makes the long *oi* sound in the words (*oy, oi*). Think of some words which contain a long *oi* sound and write them down (e.g. *boy, joy, toy, oil, soil, point*).

This is my little brother Leroy.

When Granny sees Leroy she says, "What a sweet little boy!"

When Grandpa sees Leroy he says,
"What a bundle of joy!"

But Granny and Grandpa don't know the real Leroy.

The real Leroy is an annoying
little boy.

Leroy annoys Mum. He jumps on the table.

He puts coins down the toilet.

And he has a very loud voice.

Leroy annoys my big sister.

He fiddles with her little bottles.

Leroy annoys the cat.

She thinks he is too noisy.

And Leroy annoys me!

He scribbles on
my books.

He muddles up my toys.

and pops my bubbles.

He spoils all my games.

Yes, Leroy is a destroyer!

But sometimes, just sometimes, I enjoy having a little brother.

I like to tumble about with him.

Cake

He gives me nice cuddles.

And there is one time when
Leroy isn't annoying at all.

# When he's asleep!

# Songbirds

# No Milk Today

Story by Julia Donaldson
Pictures by Jenny Williams
Series editor Clare Kirtley

**OXFORD**
UNIVERSITY PRESS

# Tips for reading No Milk Today together

This book practises these letter patterns:

ee  ea  y  e  (all pronounced *ee* as in *three*)

y  i–e  i  (all pronounced *ie* as in *tie*)

ow  o–e  o  (all pronounced *oe* as in *toe*)

ay  a–e  a  (all pronounced *ai* as in *train*)

oo  o  (all pronounced *ue* as in *blue*)

oo  oul  (all pronounced *oo* as in *good*)

ow  ou  (all pronounced *ow* as in *down*)

oi  (all pronounced *oi* as in *coin*)

Ask your child to point to these letter patterns and say the sounds (e.g. *ay* as in *today*). Look out for these letter patterns in the story.

Your child might find these words tricky:

any  can't  chased  dropped  for  give  have  her  key  many  Mr  Mrs
said  some  the  there  wants  was  were

These words are common, but your child may not have learned how to sound them out yet. Say the words for your child if they do not know them.

Before you begin, ask your child to read the title. Remind your child to read words they do not recognise by sounding out and blending. When you have finished reading the story, look through it again and:

- Ask your child, *Why did Mrs Green need the key to the shed?* (To get some hay.)
- Read pages 154 and 155. Find some words which contain a long vowel sound (*Green, snow, he, found, key, to, moo, hay*). Point to the letter pattern that makes the long vowel sound in the words (*ee, ow, e, ou, ey, o, oo, ay*).

134

Mr and Mrs Green's cat was hungry.

"Stop that noise!" said Mr Green.

Miaow!

"She just wants some milk," said
Mrs Green.

But the milk jug was empty.

"I will go and milk the cow," said
Mrs Green.

But the cow would not give any milk.

"She's hungry too," said Mrs Green.

Mrs Green went to get some hay for the cow.

But she could not open the shed. She needed a key.

"Give me the key to the shed," said
Mrs Green to Mr Green.

But Mr Green said," I can't. I dropped it in the snow."

"Go and dig the key out of the snow," said Mrs Green.

But Mr Green said, "My feet will freeze. My socks have holes in them."

"I will mend your socks," said
Mrs Green. But she could not find
any wool.

"I will get some wool from the sheep," said Mrs Green. But the sheep would not stand still.

There were too many mice running around. "I will get the cat to chase the mice away," said Mrs Green.

So Mrs Green got the cat.

The cat chased the mice. The sheep stood still.

Mrs Green got some wool. She mended
Mr Green's socks.

Mr Green dug in the snow. He found the key to the shed.

Mrs Green got the hay.

Mrs Green fed the cow. The cow gave her some milk.

"Now I can feed the cat," said
Mrs Green.

But the cat was asleep!

# Practise Your Phonics With
# Julia Donaldson's Songbirds

By the Author of The Gruffalo

## Look out for the other titles in the series …

**Top Cat and Other Stories**
978-0-19-279296-9

**The Odd Pet and Other Stories**
978-0-19-279297-6

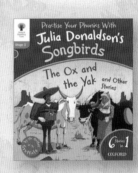

**The Ox and the Yak and Other Stories**
978-0-19-279298-3

**Scrap Rocket and Other Stories**
978-0-19-279299-0

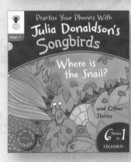

**Where is the Snail? and Other Stories**
978-0-19-279300-3

**Tadpoles and Other Stories**
978-0-19-279301-0

**My Cat and Other Stories**
978-0-19-279302-7

**Leroy and Other Stories**
978-0-19-279303-4

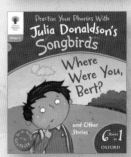

**Where Were You Bert? and Other Stories**
978-0-19-279304-1